What Do I Do...

What Do I Do...

When My Parents Fight

B. Sue Baisden

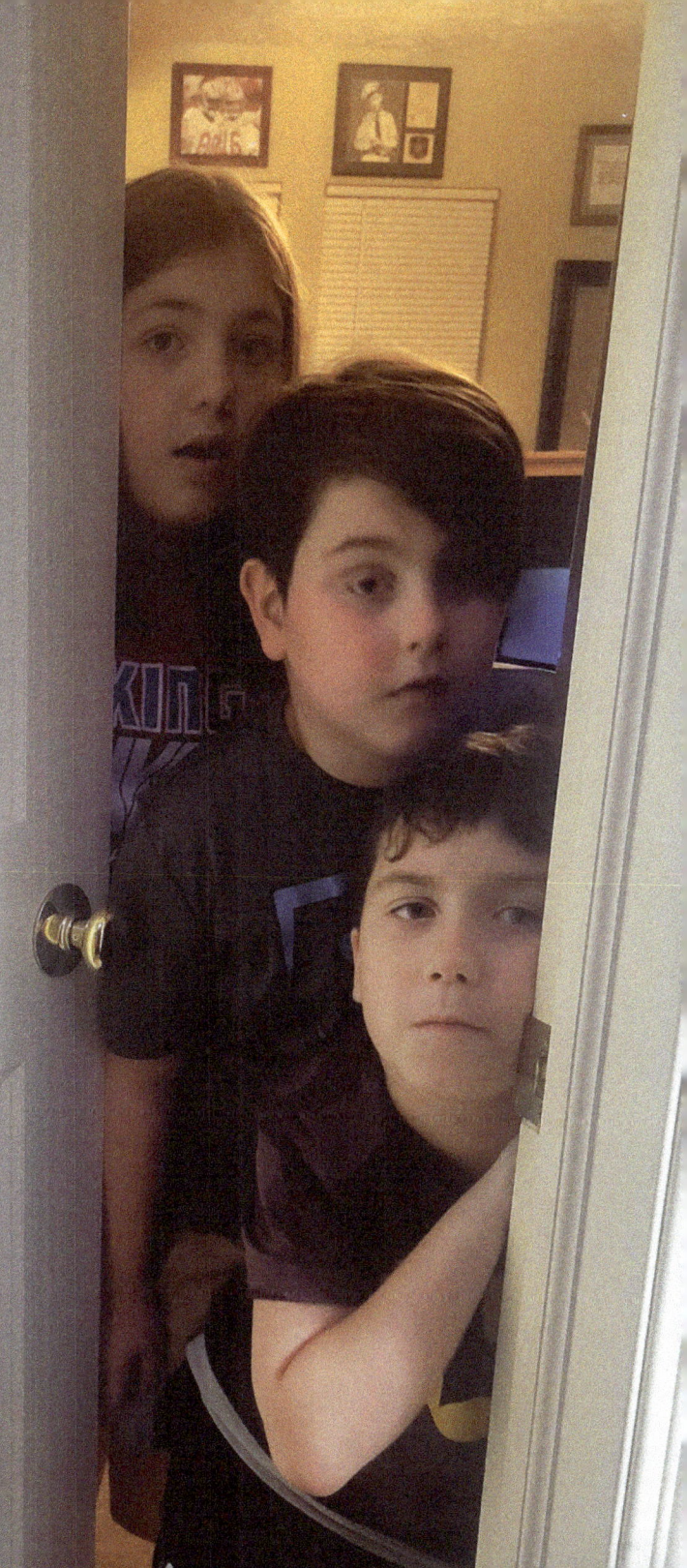

Xulon Press Elite
555 Winderley Pl, Suite 225
Maitland, FL 32751
407.339.4217
www.xulonpress.com

© 2024 by B. Sue Baisden

All rights reserved solely by the author. The author guarantees all contents are original and do not infringe upon the legal rights of any other person or work. No part of this book may be reproduced in any form without the permission of the author.

Due to the changing nature of the Internet, if there are any web addresses, links, or URLs included in this manuscript, these may have been altered and may no longer be accessible. The views and opinions shared in this book belong solely to the author and do not necessarily reflect those of the publisher. The publisher therefore disclaims responsibility for the views or opinions expressed within the work.

Paperback ISBN-13: 979-8-86850-746-5
Hardcover ISBN-13: 979-8-86850-747-2
eBook ISBN-13: 979-8-86850-748-9

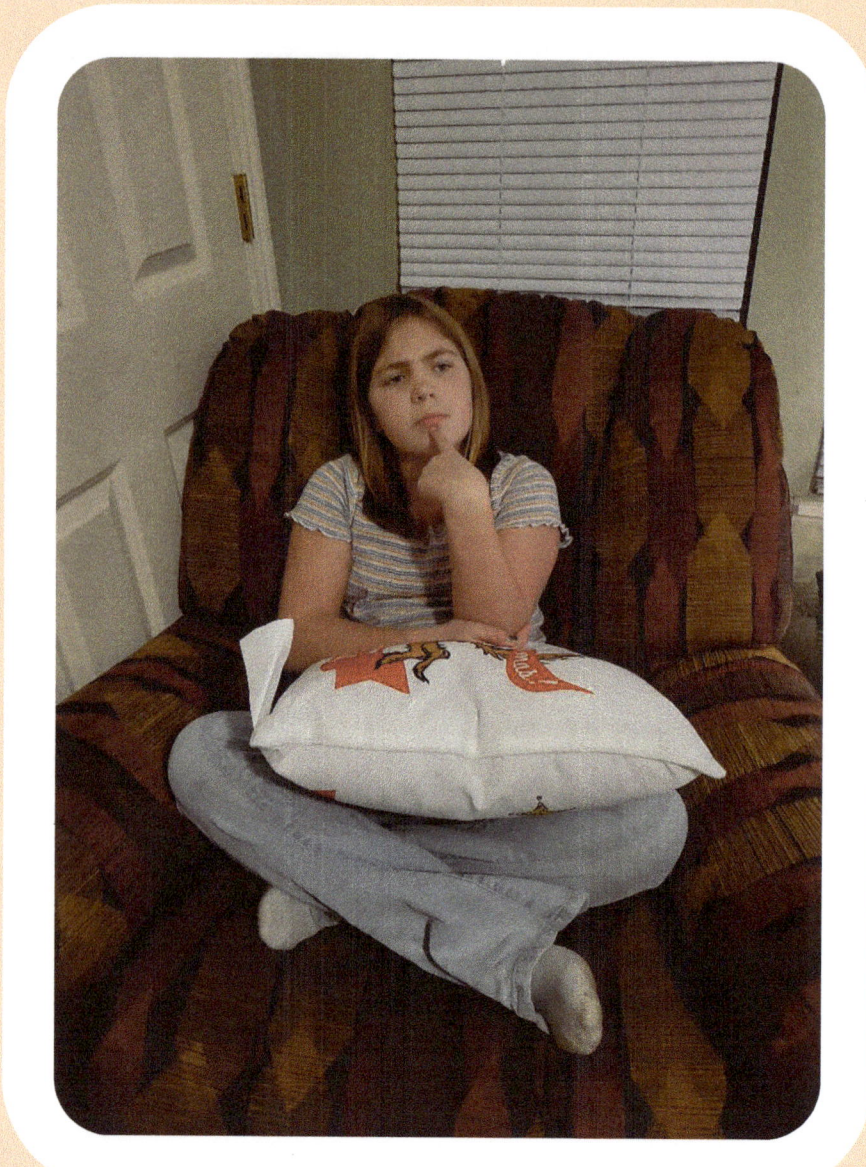

What do you do when your mom and dad fight?

When you've done everything to make it all right?

Do you run far away and pretend it's not real?

Do you hide in your room and be quiet and still?

When the yelling and cursing gets so very loud,

you cover your ears, but you can't hide the sound!

When your mom starts to cry,
and your dad starts to shout,
when maybe it's you that they're fighting about.

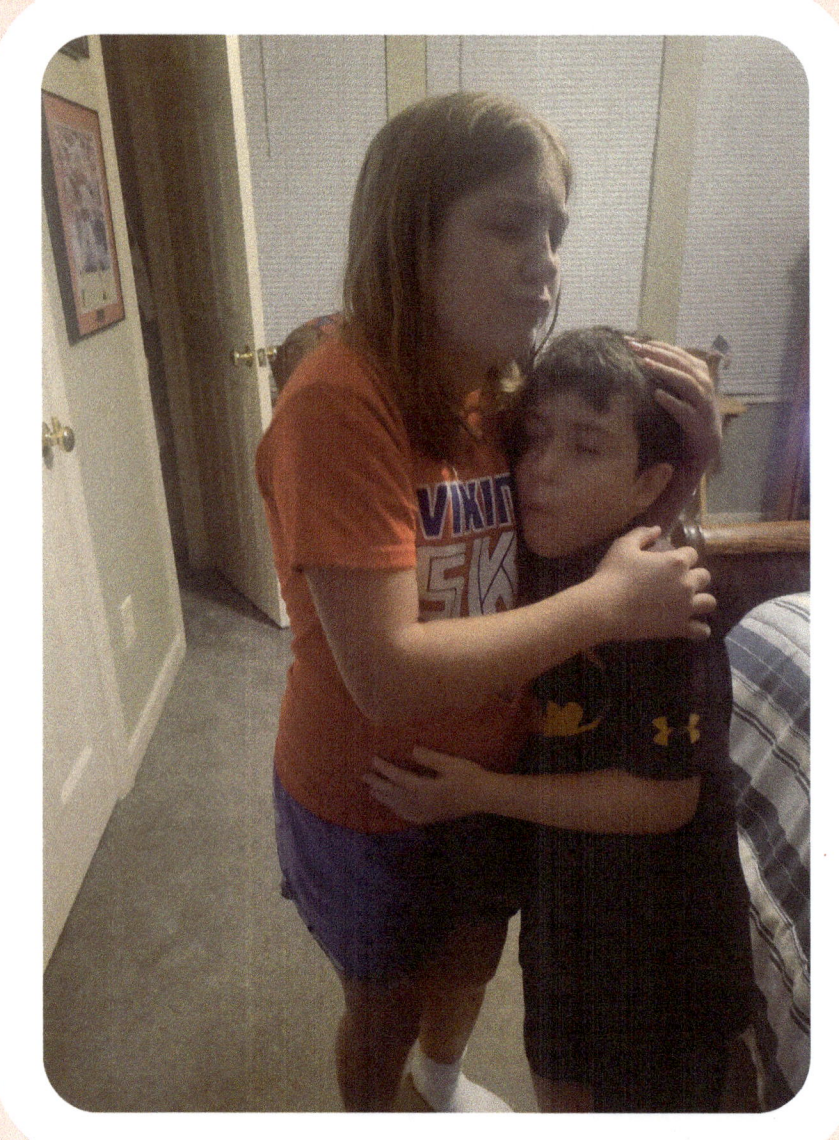

When your sister is scared and runs to you crying.

When under the bed is a good place for hiding.

When your tummy is hurting, all tied in a knot,
it makes you feel sick when they're fighting a lot.

What if he hits her? He's pounding his fist!

I heard something crash. I think it's a dish!

Should I go help her or stay in here hid?

What can I do? I'm only a kid?

I don't think their love is the same anymore.

Divorce is a word I hadn't thought of before.

I hope that our family doesn't end up this way.

I know what I'll do. I'll kneel down and pray.

Dear God, You see what my parents are doing,
how our family is hurting and needs a renewing.

I know what I'll do when the fighting won't halt.

I need to remember it isn't my fault.

God is my Father and He says in His Word
that family is special and all prayers are heard.

So, daily I'll ask Him to make a new start
to heal all the hurts and put love in their hearts.

I'll talk to my grandpa, grandma, and dad.

I'll talk to my mom, even though she is sad.

I know that the Lord will work things out fine.

Talking to Jesus helps every time!

www.ingramcontent.com/pod-product-compliance
Ingram Content Group UK Ltd.
Pitfield, Milton Keynes, MK11 3LW, UK
UKHW050626291224
453058UK00017B/126